Foreword

The ability to manage projects successfully is increasingly a source of competitive advantage for many organisations. But how can they tell how well they do this and how can they chart their improvement?

Many models have been developed to help organisations assess and enhance their performance in managing projects and programmes. The challenge is often deciding which to use.

This guide aims to provide a comparative assessment of six generic project and programme management models, based on the considered opinion of a team of leading, experienced professionals.

Each model is presented in the same structure, covering features, benefits, real-life insights and guidance on assessing the appropriateness of each.

All of the models have improvement at their heart. To improve, we must first ascertain our current capabilities and be able to compare ourselves with others, or against a standard.

That is the easy part. From there we must systematically drive up our performance to the next level so that we become measurably better.

This guide will help you take the first step – to choose a model or framework that will help you start your journey

R. Walmsl.

Sir Robert Walmsley KCB FREng

Chairman, Major Projects Association

Contents

Introduction

The guide started in 2005 as an 'APM Discovery Project' commissioned to find out more about the models on the market that claim to enable improvement in the management of projects. As a result of this research APM identified the need for a guide to provide clarity about some of the main models for APM members and other interested parties. This guide was written using the combined professional judgement of a specially selected expert panel.

There are lots of models available on the market and some have sounder foundations than others. Where does one start to find the best model for a particular situation? APM saw that there was something of value to add to the literature that already exists.

As the UK's professional body for project management, it may have been tempting to invent another model and compete with the others. However, this was deliberately resisted, choosing instead to do the hard work of clarifying six core existing models and providing advice about their purpose and use in the management of projects.

The models chosen

The featured models are:

1 Capability Maturity Model Integration (CMMI®)
2 PRINCE2™ Maturity Model (P2MM©)
3 Programme Management Maturity Model (PMMM)
4 Portfolio, Programme and Project Management Maturity Model (P3M3©)
5 Organizational Project Management Maturity Model (OPM3®)
6 Project Excellence Model

Generically, a model is a logical construct that gives some insight into a problem or area of interest. The models we feature are all designed to assess the capability, maturity or excellence of the management of projects against a defined set of criteria. Each model is also designed to suggest a road map for improvement.

APM research conducted in 2006 suggested that these models are an essential part of overall organisational effectiveness. They allow an organisation to look critically at its processes, practices and outcomes and to make plans to improve those areas that would contribute to their strategy and objectives.

All the models are applicable to the management of projects but not to individual project managers' competency; some of the models are applicable to programmes and portfolios as well as projects. In addition all the models featured are applicable to any sector irrespective of whether their history and background has a particular sector influence. This will help readers choose what's right for them, regardless of where the work started.

How to use this guide

Comparing models can be very confusing. It is difficult to decide which model would be the best fit for a particular purpose. This isn't helped by the language and abbreviations used with words like maturity, excellence and capability being used interchangeably. Whatever words are used, all imply that their use can lead to practical improvement and therefore to increased organisational value.

It may seem self-evident that the purpose of all the models is improvement, however what may be less obvious is that all of the models need to be applied with rigour and in a systematic way if measurable improvement is to be achieved over time. Experience and research have shown that when a model is not applied with full commitment from the organisation, it is likely to fail.

Whilst all of the models have an assessment framework, many different processes are used to measure the current state. For some organisations the ability to gain a 'level' or some other sort of badge is enough of a return on their investment.

For others the main value is the ability to compare with other parts of their own organisation, or to benchmark their performance against that of other organisations. Others use models to aid procurement or to demonstrate their capability when bidding for work.

Following assessment, all of the models suggest what needs to happen next to reach the next level or to improve in some other measurable way. Whether that happens is up to the organisation. All the models provide the means to improve but actual improvement clearly takes more than models and assessment.

Regardless of the model chosen, effort will be required to achieve the goals, so it is worth spending time to choose the most appropriate model and implementation approach in the first place. Our first objective is to help you choose the optimal road to take, to identify the 'staging posts' along the way and to enable project managers to gain buy-in from internal stakeholders. The initial stage can be quite a significant task in itself and we aim to make it easier. We also aim to help you see that the decision need not be a one-time choice. As you improve you may choose a different model to enable a different level or focus of improvement. As organisational needs change; so might the choice of model.

Structure of the guide

The six sections within this guide are written to the same structure to allow comparison across the models. Each model is described by exploring its features, claims and benefits with the intention of providing clarity in a practitioner-led, knowledgeable and impartial way. Case studies are included to share the experience of current users offering positive aspects of the models and areas to consider when implementing.

Most of the content of each section represents the claims made by the model 'owner', but in addition an APM verdict is provided for each model that recommends suitability for a particular purpose. You will also learn the degree to which each model can be adapted to suit particular situations and about the ability of the model to be used at a whole-organisational level, as well as applied to different business units, departments or individual programmes or projects.

In summary, the ability to deliver change is a key factor in most organisations today. The ability to deliver projects with confidence and more effectively than the competition is a source of real strategic benefit. Models to improve the management of projects can provide the route to realising tangible additional value. APM aims to demystify the subject and to speed your journey along the road to improvement.

Explanatory notes

- Improve is used as a collective term for models that encompass maturity, excellence and capability because all imply that practical improvement can be achieved, although in practice there can be a disconnect between use of models and measurable improvement if the process if not followed with rigour.

- Management of projects is used to encompass the disciplines of project, programme and portfolio management where projects must be selected and delivered within a suitable business environment. Management of projects implies involvement of the whole organisation.

- Each model description represents the claims of the model owner which have not been independently verified other than through the stated case studies.

- The language and spellings used within each model description are those specified by the model owner.

Members of the Expert Panel

Dr Terry Cooke-Davies
Professor Darren Dalcher
Adrian Dooley
Peter Easton
Neil Glover
Grahame Godding
Chris Harding
David Hinley
Carol A Long
Mary McKinlay
Ruth Murray-Webster
Mala Murton
Adrian Price
Paul Rayner
Geoff Reiss

Capability Maturity Model Integration (CMMI®)

CMMI® is owned by the Software Engineering Institute (SEI) and integrates a number of different maturity models covering the development of software, systems and hardware with the first version released in 2002. One of these models was Software CMM® which has been retired and is replaced by CMMI®.

What does it do?

CMMI® is a set of models of best practice processes for software and systems engineering. They have been developed over the years by the Software Engineering Institute (SEI) in conjunction with a number of organisations. CMMI® focuses on 'what' needs to be done rather than 'how' it should be done. Although it specifies a number of processes and practices which need to be in place, it is not generally prescriptive about how they should be carried out.

There are 22 process areas in the scope of the latest version of the model (e.g. requirements management, project planning) and each process area has a set of goals and practices associated with them.

How is it used?

The model has two different representations: staged and continuous. The staged representation has levels of maturity from 1 to 5 with each level having a number of process areas. Organisations which have not adopted process improvement programmes are typically at level 1 and progress through the levels of maturity by adopting the goals and practices which are defined for the processes at each level. All process areas within a maturity level must be assessed as conforming to achieve that level.

Staged Representation

Continuous Representation

5 Optimising
Process improvement is
a continual focus

5 Optimising

4 Quantitatively Managed
Processes are measured
and controlled

4 Quantitatively Managed

3 Defined
Processes are in place based on
an organisational standard

3 Defined

2 Managed
Basic processes are in place
but may be different by project

2 Managed

1 Initial
Processes are ad hoc,
unpredictable and reactive

1 Performed

0 Incomplete

Improved
performance
in terms of
productivity
and quality

**Specific groups of processes
assessed for maturity**

**Process areas assessed
for capability level**

figure 1 **The two representations of CMMI®**

The continuous model has the same 22 process areas, each of which can be assessed against a capability level from 0 to 5. This allows organisations to focus on the key problem process areas first or the ones which are most beneficial.

Assessments can either be conducted by the organisation itself or by employing an external appraiser. Figure 2 shows the different classes of appraisals which can be conducted which apply to either representation.

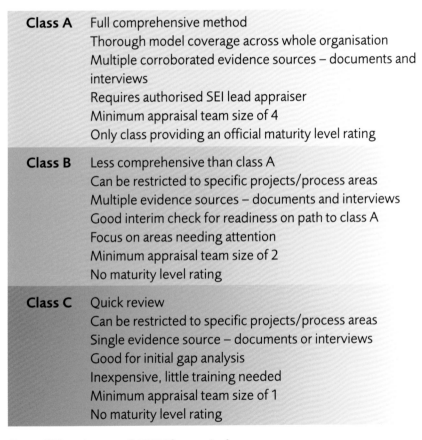

Class A   Full comprehensive method
Thorough model coverage across whole organisation
Multiple corroborated evidence sources – documents and interviews
Requires authorised SEI lead appraiser
Minimum appraisal team size of 4
Only class providing an official maturity level rating

Class B   Less comprehensive than class A
Can be restricted to specific projects/process areas
Multiple evidence sources – documents and interviews
Good interim check for readiness on path to class A
Focus on areas needing attention
Minimum appraisal team size of 2
No maturity level rating

Class C   Quick review
Can be restricted to specific projects/process areas
Single evidence source – documents or interviews
Good for initial gap analysis
Inexpensive, little training needed
Minimum appraisal team size of 1
No maturity level rating

figure 2 **The classes of CMMI® appraisal**

	self-assessed	facilitator-led	externally accredited
CMMI® Staged	Yes[1]	No	Yes
CMMI® Continuous	Yes[1]	No	Yes

[1]possible to self-assess but would need education and guidance.

Why use it?

CMMI® contains a lot of material in the public domain to enable organisations to adopt 'best practice' processes and is becoming a de facto standard. The models are not prescriptive but provide enough structure and guidance to be able to use them to good effect. Two of its strongest points are the emphasis on process improvement and institutionalisation of processes.

There are specific process areas which are dedicated to process improvement, for example, Organisational Process Focus (OPF), for planning and implementing process improvement across the organisation. In addition CMMI® defines organisational groups with practitioner involvement, such as the Engineering Process Groups (EPG), as a way of gathering requirements for process improvements and of gaining buy-in from the groups that will be affected by the changes.

Institutionalisation is one of the most difficult aspects of implementing new processes. Having embarked on a process improvement programme how do you ensure that the changes are embedded in the organisation and people won't resort to their old tried and trusted ways?

CMMI® attempts to tackle this in a number of different ways:

- Setting generic goals covering the institutionalisation of the processes;
- Gaining buy-in from the affected groups through the setting up of an EPG;
- Allowing flexibility with the ability to tailor the organisation's processes to meet individual project needs;
- Establishing measurements at a process level at level 2 maturity to assess take up and performance;
- Establishing process quality assurance at level 2 maturity to ensure adherence to standards.

Who might benefit?

The scope of CMMI® is such that most organisations with project-based developments of software or systems would benefit from adopting it as a model of best practice.

The following aspects should be noted when considering its suitability and scalability:

- Process areas outside the project life cycle are not overtly covered, for example, strategy, project portfolio management, service delivery;

- CMMI® requires formality and rigour of process which may initially add costs to an organisation's way of working; larger organisations may be better placed to make this change;

- Using the continuous model to focus on a few problem process areas first may be one way to test the water and substantiate the benefits, especially for smaller organisations where the business case is not clear;

- CMMI® can be used in conjunction with rapid methods of development, however it is process based and dictates a fair degree of rigour so the development method must be able to operate within these constraints.

Case studies

Case study 1 *Private sector*
An industrial company embarked on a wide ranging transformation of its IT organisation. One of the projects within the overall transformation programme was focused on improving its ability to deliver and maintain its business applications initially using Software CMM® (a precursor to CMMI®) and then moving to CMMI®as a model of best practice.

The project established a governance structure using a fairly standard model described by SEI: a management steering group, an Engineering Process Group (EPG) consisting of practitioners to guide and approve changes to processes and Technical Working Groups to build new processes under the direction of the EPG.

The improvements were defined and implemented using the staged representation of CMMI® with internal assessments used to monitor the progress of the improvements and level of institutionalisation between formal external assessments. Level 3 was achieved just over 2 years from the start and level 4 just over a year later.

The key benefits realised from the project were:

■ Higher productivity and quality from the use of best practice processes which are applied consistently. E.g.

  ■ Production problems reduced by over 50%;

  ■ Projects completing within their estimated effort improved from 60% to over 90%;

  ■ Projects completing to their scheduled dates improved from 70% to over 95%;

■ Higher team morale and pride in their work as a result.

The key lessons learnt from the project were:

■ Strong leadership, management ownership and focus and securing the availability of key resources are crucial to success;

■ Reusing existing assets (e.g. procedures, tools, techniques) is needed to reduce the elapsed time;

■ Process champions will help to win the hearts and minds of the practitioners using the new processes;

■ Regular communication to key stakeholders is essential to gain buy-in to the transformation.

Case study 2 *Public sector*

A public sector body employing approximately 2000 people in development adopted CMMI® to provide reassurance to their partners of their capability.

They gave a commitment to achieve a successful assessment at level 3 under a staged model. A timetable was established with milestones for the definition, implementation and embedding of level 2 and 3 processes with deadlines set for readiness for assessments. Areas to be excluded from the assessment for business reasons were described in waivers.

Senior managers were selected to lead the change on specific process areas across all projects. A team was set up to gather and promulgate good examples between different projects and to provide coaching on the details of each process area. This team also provided informal assessment of projects.

As the organisation moved towards level 2, senior management received reports of:

- Increased objectivity of reporting;
- Improved control over requirements;
- Increased control over scope creep.

The key lessons learned by the organisation:

- Reaching a CMMI® level means changing behaviour in the business;
- Senior management must run process transformation as a business change programme with time and budget;
- Senior accountability must be backed with expert resources;
- Allow time to define your own process, use the model as a guide not a template;
- Don't assume implementation equals embedding the process;
- Plan at least one internal review of a pilot process before calling it 'approved';
- Don't change all process areas in a project at once.

Further information

For further information see **www.sei.cmu.edu/cmmi/** where the CMMI® model can be downloaded free.

Verdict

APM recommends that CMMI® is used when an organisation wishes to embark on a process improvement programme covering the typical project lifecycle for development of software or systems. Where the scope includes service delivery or management processes, consider using it in conjunction with IT Infrastructure Library (ITIL®).

PRINCE2™ Maturity Model (P2MM©)

P2MM© is owned by the UK's Office of Government Commerce (OGC) and was developed in 2005-06. It is derived from OGC's Portfolio, Programme and Project Management Maturity Model (P3M3©) and Managing Successful Projects with PRINCE2™ (The PRINCE2™ Manual©). P2MM© does not itself contain detailed descriptions of the activities needed to support effective processes, as the necessary detail is contained within the PRINCE2™ Manual©.

What does it do?

P2MM© is a hierarchical model that describes the key elements of the PRINCE2™ method that need to be embedded within an organisation to achieve a certain level of maturity. The associated assessment scheme assists organisations to gauge their maturity in the use of the PRINCE2™ project management method.

The model can be used to:

- Understand the key practices that are part of an effective organisational process to manage projects;

- Identify key practices that need to be embedded within the organisation to achieve the next level of maturity;

- Understand the rationale behind the assessment questionnaire.

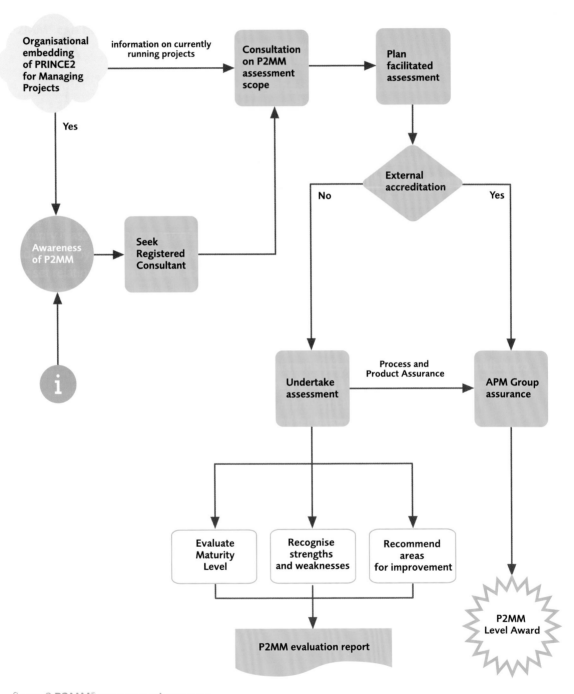

figure 2 **P2MM©assessment process**

Why use it?

A P2MM© assessment can be undertaken for an organisation that delivers projects internally or in organisations that provide a project management service to other organisations.

The main benefit for organisations that deliver internal projects is that they will be able to identify their strengths and areas for improvement and construct an action plan to improve their effectiveness in the use of PRINCE2™. This will lead to PRINCE2™being embedded within the organisation and delivery of the full benefits of using a structured project management method.

There are additional benefits for organisations providing a project management service, in that they will also be able to provide evidence to their clients and prospective clients of their level of maturity in the use of PRINCE2™. This could provide a distinct marketing advantage.

Who might benefit?

Any organisation using PRINCE2™ as the standard project management method for their projects could benefit from P2MM© and its associated assessment scheme.

The assessment process is designed with scalability in mind, i.e. APM Group Ltd has issued explicit guidance on the number of project sponsors and project managers to be interviewed, depending upon the number of discrete projects running in the organisation. P2MM© is particularly suitable to those organisations that use PRINCE2™ for project management and are considering or are undertaking wider scale maturity level evaluations of not only project management, but programme and portfolio management using P3M3©.

Case studies

Case study 1 *Public sector*
The head of IT at a relatively new public sector organisation, perceived the need for a greater degree of governance of IT projects. It was decided that P3M3© accreditation would be undertaken to baseline the current processes and help determine the course of action to embed and improve processes.

As the organisation had decided to adopt the PRINCE2™ method for project management, a preliminary marker was obtained through a project management capability assessment using P2MM©.

" The organisation has had to grow fast and change quickly. It is a common mistake for organisations to think they just need to send staff on training courses and a new process will then be adopted. Everyone will use their own interpretation of the method and bolt it onto existing processes."

Programme manager

The organisation achieved a P2MM© assessment of Level 3, only the second organisation worldwide to achieve this level.

The programme manager commented:

" We can prove to everyone that we are doing a proficient job right now."

Having undertaken a process capability assessment, the organisation has established a continual improvement process to ensure they continue to mature. They intend to track their progress through future P3M3© assessments.

Public sector efficiency is the spotlight of public interest. For an organisation that has been set up specifically to pay compensation to people if their pension scheme collapses, being able to demonstrate that they continue to manage projects effectively is very important.

Case study 2 *Private sector*

A project and programme management review of procedures and working practices was being undertaken at a telecommunications company. This coincided with the publication of the draft version of P2MM© and after attending a training course, the consultant in charge decided to apply the model as part of the overall health-check.

The review indicated that only 24% of projects were being delivered on time with 50% of projects taking twice as long as planned. Consequently, morale had been affected and although tools and techniques were available they were not being used effectively.

As a result of the review, the business decided that it was imperative to build capability in a number of areas, including project management. A 'best practice' project was established, that aimed amongst other things, to achieve Level 3 (P2MM©) within a year.

The organisation went on to embed repeatable, documented processes based on the PRINCE2™ method. The commitment from senior management provided the necessary organisational focus, so that responsibility for improving the organisation's overall project management capability was defined, lessons learned and the culture transformed.

The consultant commented the key outcomes within the year were:

- Better project management morale;
- Improvement in project success in terms of time and cost indicators.

A key aspect of achieving Level 3 was the ability to flex the centrally controlled project processes to suit particular project needs. In this way the organisation could integrate the method with the organisation processes, e.g. for business planning, bid management and commercial management.

The maturity model approach provided a suitable framework for continuous improvement and support – in terms of a 'centre of excellence', quality assurance and proactive problem management.

Further information

For further information about P2MM© contact OGC Service Desk

Tel: 0845 000 4999
email: ServiceDesk@ogc.gsi.gov.uk
Web: www.ogc.gsi.gov.uk

or APM Group Ltd, who administer the P2MM© assessment scheme,

Tel: 01494 452450
email: info@apmgroup.co.uk

Portfolio, Programme and Project Management Maturity Model (P3M3©), version 1.0, Feb. 2006. Available for free download from the OGC website.

PRINCE2™ Maturity Model (P2MM©), version 1.0, March 2006. Available for free download from the OGC website.

Managing Successful Projects with PRINCE2™ (the PRINCE2™ Manual 2005). OGC – Published by the Stationary Office, May 2005. ISBN 10 0113309465.

Verdict

APM recommends that P2MM© is used when an organisation has chosen PRINCE2™ as a project management method and wishes to evaluate the extent to which PRINCE2™ is embedded throughout the organisation's projects.

P2MM©, having been derived from the more comprehensive P3M3©, can be used with P3M3© assessments to cover wider aspects of portfolio, programme and project management.

The Programme Management Maturity Model (PMMM)

PMMM is owned by two of the APM Programme Management (ProgM) specific interest group officers, Paul Rayner and Geoff Reiss. It was developed and published into the public domain in 2000 to provide a benchmarking facility for programme management teams.

PMMM is a true benchmarking tool as it allows organisations to compare their programmes with other programmes in an international database. Programmes in this context are co-ordinated groups of projects intended together to deliver change of strategic significance.

ProgM is an APM specific interest group that maintains working relationships with other organisations, including the British Computer Society (BCS), the Project Management Institute (PMI). The database of models is collected and maintained by ProgM on a voluntary basis. Use of the PMMM is free.

What does it do?

PMMM examines programmes using ten key aspects of programme management and is linked to the Programme Management Improvement Process that provides a guide to improving maturity across these areas.

PMMM provides a mechanism for benchmarking and comparing an organisation's maturity across the ten aspects of programme management at the level of a single programme, a group of programmes or a complete organisation, and against a substantial and growing database of similar models.

The ten aspects of programme management covered by PMMM are:

1   Management organisation;

2   Planning;

3   Management of benefits;

4   Management of stakeholders;

5   Issue and risk management;

6   Quality management and auditing;

7   Configuration management;

8   Internal communication;

9   Programme accounting and finances;

10 Scope and change.

The simple process delivers a report showing the candidate's maturity in the ten aspects and the average of all the other models in the database at the time of analysis. Through special comparisons made by request, programmes may be compared with sub-sets of the databank such as other public sector programmes, UK programmes, IT programmes, etc.

At the time of writing, the database contains data based on the analysis of over 150 programmes from a wide range of organisations across the world.

How is it used?

PMMM can be used by a specific programme manager or a group across an organisation and may be used as a self-assessment tool or by independent analysis.

PMMM may be used on either a self-assessed or facilitator-led basis. There are no particular training or accreditation requirements for assessors, although they should be knowledgeable about contemporary programme management and comply with the conditions of use which are contained on the data collection form.

	self-assessed	facilitator-led	externally accredited
PMMM	**Yes**	**Yes**	**No**

The data collection form can be downloaded from the ProgM website **(www.e-programme.com).**

The form asks some background questions about the organisation, its industry and size. This information is used for statistical analysis. It then requests answers to 60 statements: six for each of the ten key aspects of programme management.

To complete a form, each statement is evaluated by ticking one of three boxes. For example one of the 60 questions is reproduced below:

Question	None	Partly	Fully
The roles and responsibilities of component project/work-stream managers are defined and agreed.	☐	☐	☐

The process of submitting completed forms to ProgM for analysis is explained in the form itself. Completed forms, once received are entered into a database by members of ProgM and a response is generated.

A typical response will contain:

- Numerical assessment of the maturity of the organisation's programme management in each of the ten key aspects;

- A graphic profile of the programmes, showing comparisons with other programmes in the database;

- Expert comment and assessment.

A typical graphic profile is shown below:

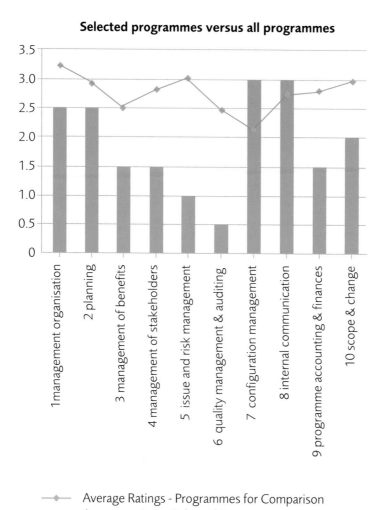

Selected programmes versus all programmes

— Average Ratings - Programmes for Comparison
▬ Average ratings - Selected Programmes

figure1 **Selected programmes versus all programmes**

Why use it?

PMMM allows an organisation or the management of a specific programme to understand its strengths and weaknesses in programme management maturity in comparison with other organisations. This helps an organisation to prioritise and plan improvements. PMMM may be used to compare programmes against each other, organisations against other organisations or to measure improvements over time. The Programme Management Improvement Process published in *The Gower Handbook of Programme Management* (see further information) provides guidance on prioritising and implementing improvements to maturity.

Who might benefit?

Any organisation that uses programme management to deliver change of strategic significance would benefit from using PMMM to benchmark their current maturity.

The model has been used on specific programmes, comparing specific programmes over time, comparing department and divisions of a single organisation and across the whole organisation. Furthermore, data is available within the database to allow comparison with other programmes in specific industry sectors (IT, banking, public sector, etc.) and geographies (e.g. UK, US, etc.).

Case studies

Case study 1 *Private sector*
A major Dutch insurance company used PMMM to analyse its portfolio of 15 large, organisational change programmes. Under the guidance of an external consultant, individual questionnaires were completed by each programme manager.

These were analysed and consolidated to give an overall view of the state of programme management maturity within the organisation and to compare it with that of finance organisations in general. In addition, a one-to-one feedback session was held with each programme manager to identify possible avenues for improvement.

The end result was a road map for individual and collective programme improvement. Commenting on this, the director with responsibility for programme management noted in December 2005 that the exercise had been 'extremely valuable' and had 'helped to focus all involved on exploiting opportunities for practical improvement.'

Case study 2 *Public sector*

PMMM was used by a Canadian University as a key analytical tool within a management development programme. Participants used it to analyse programmes within their organisations and then to discuss the findings with colleagues so as to identify best practice that could be adopted.

One outcome was to identify that several initiatives that had been described as programmes were, in fact, projects and thus produced unusual profiles.

Speaking of the results, the professor in charge of the analysis commented in May 2004 that 'I am certain that the programme management maturity questionnaire will contribute significantly to our discussions.'

Further information

Visit the ProgM website **www.e-programme.com/pmmm.**

Reiss, G. and Rayner, P et al. *The Gower Handbook of Programme Management*, Gower Publishing Limited 2006, ISBN 0-566-08603-4

Verdict

APM recommends that PMMM is used when organisations seek to prioritise and plan improvements to the management, governance or reporting of their programmes of business change.

PMMM is aimed at programmes and therefore is not appropriate for specific projects. Being comparative in nature it has exceptional strengths in comparative analysis of programmes and organisations.

PMMM analyses maturity in ten key aspects and it has specific strengths in highlighting weaker aspects of programme management where an organisation may gain rapid benefits through improvements.

Portfolio, Programme and Project Management Maturity Model (P3M3©)

P3M3© is owned by the Office of Government Commerce (OGC) and was developed in 2004 to build programme and portfolio maturity elements into an existing project management maturity model. It is currently under review to take account of recent changes in OGC guidance on risk, programme and portfolio management.

What does it do?

The P3M3© is essentially a set of structured descriptions of some 32 processes that span project, programme and portfolio management e.g. project definition, risk management and quality management (see figure 1).

Processes	Maturity Levels
Project definition Programme management awareness	1
Business case development Programme organisation Programme definition Project establishment Project planning, monitoring & control Stakeholder management & communications Requirements management Risk management Configuration management Programme planning & control Management of suppliers & external parties	2
Benefits management Transition management Information management Organisational focus Process definition Training, skills & competency development Integrated management & reporting Life cycle control Inter-group co-ordination & networking Quality assurance Centre of Excellence (COE) role deployment Organisation portfolio establishment	3
Management metrics Quality management Organisational cultural growth Capacity management	4
Proactive problem management Technology management Continuous process improvement	5

figure 1 **Processes under each maturity level**

The process descriptions are allotted within the document structure to five different maturity levels from the lowest 'Initial Process' through 'Repeatable Process', 'Defined Process' and 'Managed Process' to the highest 'Optimised Process'.

This model is based on the process maturity framework that was developed into the Software Engineering Institute's (SEI) Capability Maturity Model. SEI has further developed their framework into the Capability Maturity Model Integration (CMMI®) set of models.

While this is a model that OGC developed to be compatible with its family of guidance (PRINCE2™, Managing Successful Programmes and Management of Risk) it was designed for use in a generic portfolio management environment and does not assess directly against these specific methods.

How is it used?

P3M3© provides a description of what 'good' looks like for the representative processes at each level of maturity. It does not include any self-service analytical tools and is best used by an independent expert who can make judgements of how well the existing processes in the organisation stand up against the model process descriptions.

	Project Management		Programme Management		Portfolio Management
	Organisation	Delivery	Organisation	Delivery	Organisation
Head of Projects	✔				
Head of Projects Office	✔				
Project Sponsor	✔	✔			
Project Manager		✔			
Head of Programmes and Projects	✔		✔		
Head of Programmes Office	✔		✔		
Senior Responsible Owner (SRO)			✔	✔	
Business Change Manager			✔	✔	
Programme Manager				✔	
Portfolio Director					✔
Head of Centre of Excellence (or equivalent)	✔		✔		✔

figure 2 **Example interview list**

The APM Group provides a service to accredit consultants as competent users of P3M3©. Typically, the consultants will interview key PPM stakeholders, using a set of standard questions, and plot the answers against the P3M3© model.

An example of an interview list is shown in figure 2. The analysis results in an assessment of the organisation's overall level of competence. Rating at a level requires a satisfactory assessment of all the processes at that level and all lower levels. Because an assessment rates the organisation's capabilities for each individual process it helps to identify specific areas requiring improvement.

	self-assessed	facilitator-led	externally accredited
P3M3©	**No**	**Yes**	**Yes**

Why use it?

P3M3© will be of interest to any organisation that is concerned about the quality and effectiveness of its programme/project delivery. It provides a means to measure existing capabilities and identify areas for improvement.

The levels in the model indicate the progression of capability requirements from managing reasonably simple projects to becoming a flexible and highly-skilled portfolio management organisation. Not every organisation needs to attain level 5 and current experience suggests that level 3 is a minimum to aim for, although most organisations would only currently only rate a level 2.

Organisations may use this form of analysis in a variety of ways:

- The accredited consultancy service provides an independent assessment of current capabilities. This can answer the question 'Are we good enough at what we do?'

- The model can be used to compare current competence levels with those that would be required to expand the organisation into a more complex project management environment or to test the competencies of a new organisation.

- Because the model associates processes with levels of competence, it can be used to help identify particular skills weaknesses that are inhibiting overall performance levels. For example, if the organisation would have expected a level 3 rating but had poorly implemented information management and quality assurance processes, then there is a clearly defined development need.

- An organisation whose business is the provision of programme and project management services can use the assessment as proof of competence for its clients. Conversely the model can be used to specify competence requirements for buying in programme and project management services

- The assessment can be used to inform a risk assessment of a new programme or project in the organisation by identifying the areas where capabilities are weak and hence where additional training or use of external resources would be required to mitigate the risks.

The use of skilled and accredited external assessors provides the organisation with a realistic assessment of its own levels of competence across its project, programme and portfolio management landscape. An initial assessment within an organisation can be used in future as a benchmark. It can also be used to assess the effectiveness of actions taken to improve processes within the organisation.

Who might benefit?

The model is designed to help assess corporate capabilities but its real benefit is in improving project delivery and in reducing capability-based risks to the management of the organisation's overall portfolio of projects.

The beneficiaries are:

- The board of management. They will be better informed of the organisation's ability to deliver its portfolio of programmes and projects.

- The head of the programme/project management unit or centre of excellence. The analysis provides information to identify the priority areas for improvement for the overall portfolio management capabilities of the organisation.

Case study

Even though the P3M3° model has been in existence for some time, the accredited consultancy service is relatively new and, unlike the project management maturity models, there is little case study material that encompasses programme and portfolio management assessments.

Case study *Public sector*

The first organisation to achieve a P3M3° accreditation was the Pension Protection Fund (PPF). This was a new public corporation established to assess and pay compensation when employers go bust, leaving large deficits in their defined benefit pension schemes.

As such it has had a high public profile and needed to get things right from the outset. PPF achieved a level 3 rating with the PRINCE2$^{™}$ Maturity Model but the head of the organisation's programme management office was keen to establish a programme management ethos and sought a P3M3° assessment on setting up the Programme Management Office (PMO).

The PPF is pleased with getting a P3M3° accreditation: "Because we have proven our capability it gives us the confidence and authority to know we are running operations professionally. We can prove to everyone that not only are we doing a proficient job right now but also show we have a continual improvement process in place to ensure we continue to mature as an organisation."

But PPF believes the real benefit is in the assessment process itself. "It's not the accreditation that matters it's the journey and it's really about a commitment to working as a team, encouraging and leading the organisation without having to push anyone into doing tasks they don't understand. Although it can be hard work, ultimately, adopting a PPM framework is empowering for everyone."

In this case this is not a large organisation with a complex portfolio of major projects and programmes, but a new and tightly focused public body. The benefits of using the maturity model were in building confidence within the programme delivery team and to their management that they have the capability to deliver a new and politically sensitive service.

Further information

For further information contact OGC Service Desk
Tel: 0845 000 4999
email: ServiceDesk@ogc.gsi.gov.uk
Web: www.ogc.gsi.gov.uk

or APM Group Ltd, who administer the P3M3© Accreditation Service,
Tel: 01494 452450
email: info@apmgroup.co.uk

Portfolio, Programme and Project Management Maturity Model (P3M3©), version 1.0, Feb. 2006. Available for free download from the OGC website.

PRINCE2™ Maturity Model (P2MM©), version 1.0, March 2006. Available for free download from the OGC website.

Verdict

APM recommends that P3M3© is used when an organisation desires to evaluate the existing project management process capability and may wish to either repeat the exercise to evaluate their improvement actions or wish to extend the scope to include programme and portfolio management in a seamless manner using one assessment scheme.

Organizational Project Management Maturity Model *(OPM3®)*

OPM3® is a standard owned by the Project Management Institute (PMI) and was launched in December 2003 to help organizations align diverse aspects of their operations with their overall business strategy.

What does it do?

The application of *OPM3* assists organizations in establishing policies and process standards to ensure that operations are consistent with strategic objectives.

The standard defines organizational project management as, "the application of knowledge, skills, tools and techniques to organizational and project activities to achieve the aims of an organization through projects."

Organizational project management maturity is consequently defined as the extent to which an organization practices organizational project management.

The scope of the standard encompasses those processes that it deems necessary in order to manage the three domains of portfolios, programs and projects, the relationship between which is portrayed in figure 1.

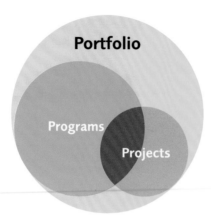

figure 1 **Programs and projects are part of a project portfolio**

The standard defines globally developed and recognised industry 'best practices' that are necessary in each of these three domains, and the incremental 'capabilities' that are prerequisites to each 'best practice'. Both the term 'best practice' and the term 'capability' are defined within the standard. The degree to which each 'capability' is practiced is defined in terms of one of four stages of process improvement: standardised, controlled, measured or improved.

How is it used?

OPM3 can be thought of as consisting of three inter-locking elements: knowledge, assessment and improvement. The *OPM3® Knowledge Foundation* describes the contents of the standard, which can be used as the basis initially for assessing the degree of organizational project management maturity and subsequently for identifying those improvements that are felt to be necessary. There are thus many ways that the model can be used.

The recommendation within the standard is that a continuous improvement cycle is employed consisting of five stages:

- Prepare for assessment using the *OPM3® Knowledge Foundation;*

- Perform an assessment;

- Plan for improvements;

- Implement improvements;

- Repeat the cycle (until satisfied with the results).

Assessments can be performed in different ways, for example:

■ The standard contains a 'self-assessment module' (SAM) consisting of 151 questions, each of which is to be answered 'yes' or 'no'. The SAM both gives an indicative 'score', and points to those capabilities that do not appear to be fully implemented;

■ A detailed assessment can be carried out using the performance indicators associated with each capability within the *OPM3® Knowledge Foundation*. This gives a more detailed indication of organizational project management maturity, but can only be accessed through the SAM once an assessment has been completed;

■ An external assessment can be conducted by a PMI Certified *OPM3®* Assessor™ using *OPM3®* ProductSuite. This is an evidence-based assessment that uses both interviews and reviews of documentation to ensure the existence and the extent of implementation of the processes. It uses formal protocols, and an automated capability-level assessment to measure the actual maturity in terms of the standard.

	self-assessed	facilitator-led	externally accredited
OPM3®	**Yes**	**Optional**	**No**
OPM3® ProductSuite	**No**	**Yes**	**Yes**

Similarly, there are different ways of identifying desirable improvements, for example:

■ Using the indicative score from the SAM, the organization can simply decide which areas seem to it to be most in need of improvement;

■ Using an external facilitator or consultant, the organization can use the results of a detailed capabilities assessment to target specific areas for improvement;

■ Using a PMI Certified *OPM3®* Consultant™ an improvement tool that relates improvements to the organizational strategy and that is built into *OPM3®* ProductSuite.

Why use it?

The benefits claimed for *OPM3* are that it:

- Bridges the gap between strategy and individual projects;

- Provides a comprehensive body of knowledge regarding what constitutes best practice in organizational project management;

- Enables an organization to determine precisely what capabilities it does and doesn't have – in other words its degree of maturity;

- Provides guidance for prioritising and planning improvements.

Who might benefit?

Organizations of all sizes, in all three sectors, and in any industry could benefit from *OPM3* if they are serious about embedding into their business the necessary processes to link strategy to projects. It is probably best suited to organizations that are committed to organization-wide improvement (either in a discrete business unit or department, or enterprise wide) and that have already started on the journey of improving organizational project management.

It will be particularly appealing to organizations in which the language of PMI's *PMBOK® Guide* is already common currency.

PMI has announced its intention of incorporating its standards for portfolio management and program management into a second edition, probably due to be published in 2008.

Case studies

Case study 1 *Private sector*

An old-established US Industrial Corporation employing some 10,000 people on a single (large) site in the provision of services to a US Government Department had decided to apply project management techniques throughout its entire business, operations as well as projects. It had adopted a "nested" approach of locating programmes within portfolios, and projects within programmes. The structure of programmes was aligned with the structure of its contract with the US Government.

Believing that project management success was driven by a combination of individual competence and organizational maturity, the organization decided to carry out a comprehensive *OPM3* assessment, using externally-accredited facilitators.

More than 20 site staff were interviewed, and the organization's project documentation and records were examined.

The key benefits of the assessment were:

- Confirmation that the organization's project management processes were very mature;

- Identification of specific opportunities for improvement in, for example, the program level conduct of procurement and risk management;

- Identification of specific opportunities to strengthen already impressive project management practices.

As a result of the assessment, the organization established a 'Program Improvement Team' to develop and implement appropriate processes and disciplines.

Case study 2 *Public sector*

An international firm of management consultants had been retained by the project management office of a Mid-Eastern government department to develop and implement new programme and portfolio management practices and processes.

At the start of the activity, it was decided to undertake an *OPM3* assessment of the maturity of the current project, programme and portfolio practices both to provide a baseline against which to measure improvements, and to provide indications of which specific improvements would provide the greatest 'leverage'.

The key benefits of the assessment were:

- Recognition of improvements that can be made to existing project management processes by the development and implementation of systems to control them;

- Identification of a small number of key management areas, the improvement of which would result in a significant improvement in maturity overall;

- Confirmation of the need for the proposed new programme and portfolio practices.

The intention is to repeat the assessment after the implementation of the new practices in order to demonstrate the improvements that have been made.

Further information

For further information contact Project Management Institute Inc., Four Campus Boulevard, Newtown Square, PA 19073-3299 USA, or visit **www.pmi.org**

Verdict

APM recommends that *OPM3* is used when organizations are serious about making root and branch process improvements to link strategy to projects, especially if PMI's other standards are widely known within the organization. For further information contact the Project Management Institute.

Project Excellence Model

The Project Excellence Model is owned by the International Project Management Association (IPMA) and was developed in 1996 by the German Project Management Association from the European Foundation for Quality Management (EFQM) Excellence Model. The EFQM Excellence Model and the Project Excellence Model appear similar, but the former is concerned with assessing excellence of processes within a business, whereas the Project Excellence Model is concerned with assessing the excellence of delivery of a single project.

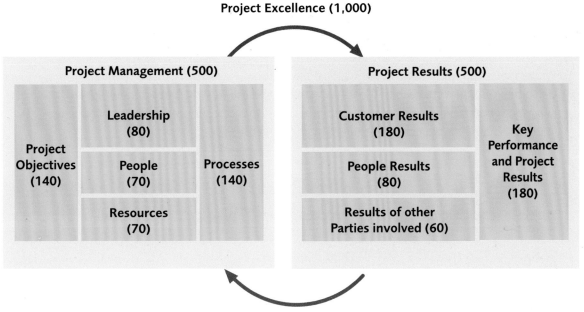

Project Excellence (1,000)

Project Management (500)

Project Objectives (140)

Leadership (80)

People (70)

Resources (70)

Processes (140)

Project Results (500)

Customer Results (180)

People Results (80)

Results of other Parties involved (60)

Key Performance and Project Results (180)

figure 1 **The Project Excellence Model**

The arrow at the top emphasises the cause and effect between management and results, and the arrow at the bottom the link to learning from experience and the constant improvement elements of the model.

What does it do?

The Project Excellence Model provides a framework for assessing how well a project team is delivering, or has delivered a project. The nine criteria shown on the model in figure 1 are sub-divided into 22 sub-criteria, and each of these is described in a way that allows actual activities and results to be assessed. The descriptions of the criteria enable an appropriate starting point for assessment to be chosen depending on the type of project. The model is used systematically by review of the project against each of the criteria, assessing whether or not the project has sound processes in place to achieve results.

The model is based on the assumption that projects are driven by their Objectives. The first criterion therefore examines the way in which the project has defined the objectives, identified stakeholders and managed the objectives throughout the project. To achieve the defined objectives, the project team carry out project management that enables project results. Leadership, People, Resources and Processes are enabling aspects of project management and the model looks for a strong cause and effect between the excellence of project management across all of these areas and actual project results. Project results, or the outcomes of project management include Customer Results, People Results and the Results of Other Parties Involved, as well as Key Performance and Project Results. The Key Performance and Project Results section is directly looking for alignment with the Objectives.

How is it used?

The model is applied to a single project or a group of projects making up a portfolio. Using the descriptors of each of the 22 sub-criteria and the scoring protocol, scores are awarded for each project being assessed. In addition to the scores; strengths and areas for improvement of the project are identified to underpin the scoring.

	self-assessed	facilitator-led	externally accredited
Project Excellence Model	**Yes**	**Yes**	**No**[1]

[1] but is used as the model by IPMA for the annual International Project Excellence Awards.

The model is available for anyone to use but requires assessors who have been trained by IPMA to interpret the criteria and provide consistent scores.

Organisations that enter particular projects into the annual International Project Excellence Awards will be assessed by a team of external assessors. The first stage is for each individual assessor to review the project documentation and perform an evaluation. At the next stage of the assessment process, the team evaluating the project bring their scores together and are required to achieve consensus on the level of scoring of each of the sub-criteria. This is aggregated into an overall project score using the relative weighting assigned to each criterion. Award applicants, whose projects achieve a sufficiently high overall score, are visited by the assessment team to allow further clarification of the claims of the project in their application document.

The final output is a feedback report which provides an explanation of the basis for the scoring and identifies the strengths of the project and the areas for further development and the planned improvement actions.

The process used for awards can be adapted so that the model can be used as a tool for self-assessment or external assessment of a project. In any case, it is designed to be used as part of a comprehensive, systematic and regular review process, by which an organisation would be able to clearly identify strengths and highlight areas in which improvements to the management of projects can be made.

Why use it?

IPMA claim the following benefits for the Project Excellence Model:

- The model provides an evidence-based structured approach to the assessment of projects, which is both scalable and repeatable;

- The measurement of performance within their own projects can offer the organisation confidence that the processes, behaviours and systems they have introduced are working effectively as part of the project management framework;

- Feedback from the assessment identifies strengths and areas for improvement for individual projects and the organisation as a whole;

- Involvement in the assessment process gives those involved a critical insight into how their projects are managed and how they can be improved;

- The project excellence score establishes the organisation's position in its progress towards excellence in the field of project management.

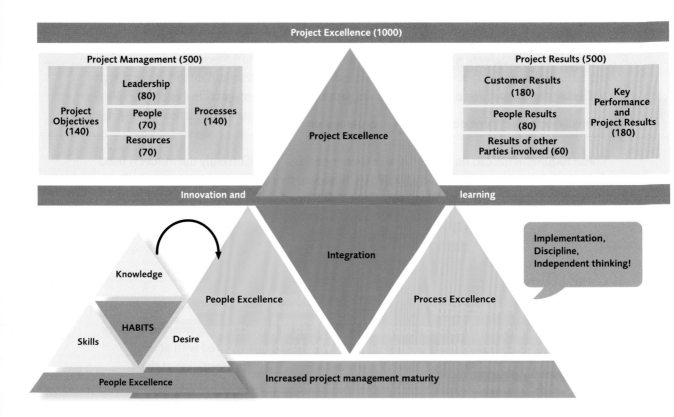

Source: Dr Frank Menter, Erwin Weitlaner   ©Siemens AG 2007 Siemens Transportation systems

figure 3 **Example of Project Excellence Model integrated into an organisation's strategy.**

Case study 2 *Public sector*

A national utility corporation in India is concerned with major projects in the field of Power Generation. The CEO recently described the impact of using the Project Excellence Model for their entries in the IPMA Awards in the following terms;

"The award and use of the model has created a different outlook in project management. There is a realisation that we had to do something better than we used to do. Innovation has become a key word in the management of projects. As a result we have been able to set national benchmarks for our activities."

Further information

For further information contact the IPMA awards at **info@ipma.ch**

International Project Management Association, 2006, IPMA Awards, Award Model, viewed: 30 October 2006 **www.ipma.ch/asp/default.asp?p=165**

Verdict

APM recommends that the Project Excellence Model is used for evaluating a single project as a means of identifying project management related strengths and areas for improvement. It is of most value when used for comparative analysis of projects within a programme or portfolio, or as an internal or external benchmark.

Index

Association for Project Management

Who we are

The Association for Project Management (APM) is the largest professional body of its kind in Europe. The association represents over 15,300 individual and 450 corporate members. At its heart is the *APM Body of Knowledge;* a comprehensive resource outlining the 52 knowledge areas required to manage all projects in all sectors.

APM is dedicated to the development of project professionals; recognising the growing requirement to deliver managed change effectively. Project professionals have the skills, resources, expertise and attitude that ensure projects are delivering the required benefits.

What we do

APM is a recognised authority, working to ensure the professional discipline of project management is developed for the public good.

This is achieved through an internationally recognised four level qualification structure for all levels of project capability, from introduction to senior project professionals. APM also has a pan-sector membership of project professionals developing their careers through regional branches, Specific Interest Groups and access to knowledge resources such as *Project* magazine and the *APM Body of Knowledge 5th edition.*

The *APM Body of Knowledge,* APM Publishing and APM Project Management Conference all contribute to the national and international project management agenda through discussion, debate and thought leadership.

About this guide

APM is dedicated to the development of project and programme management performance. This guide has been developed using the combined expertise of APM members, who are all recognised authorities in their field. APM has helped to fund, manage and promote the writing and production of this guide.

To join APM or for information please contact:

Association for Project Management, 150 West Wycombe Road, High Wycombe, HP12 3AE
Tel: 0845 458 1944, Fax: 01494 523 937, Email: **info@apm.org.uk**, Web: **www.apm.org.uk**